This book belongs to

_____

WHITE STAR PUBLISHERS

Contents

Before I arrived

My parents found out about my arrival when

This is what Mama told Papa:

This is how Papa reacted:

The date of my expected birth was

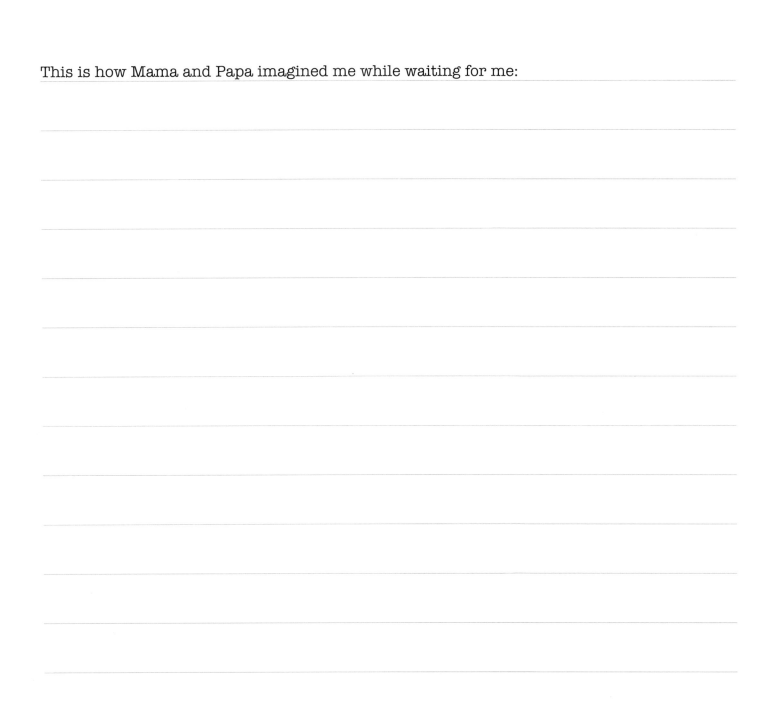

This is how Mama and Papa imagined me while waiting for me:

In Mama's big tummy

My parents heard my heartbeat for the first time

Mama felt me kick for the first time

While waiting for me, Mama always had a craving for

My family made important preparations before my arrival, such as:

THE FIRST ECHOGRAPH

My family

Mama's name is

Her dream for me is

Papa's name is

His dream for me is

The other members of my family

Some information about my family

Mama's family tree

COUSINS

COUSINS

COUSINS

COUSINS

MAMA

UNCLES

UNCLES

AUNTS

AUNTS

GRAND-MOTHER

GRAND-FATHER

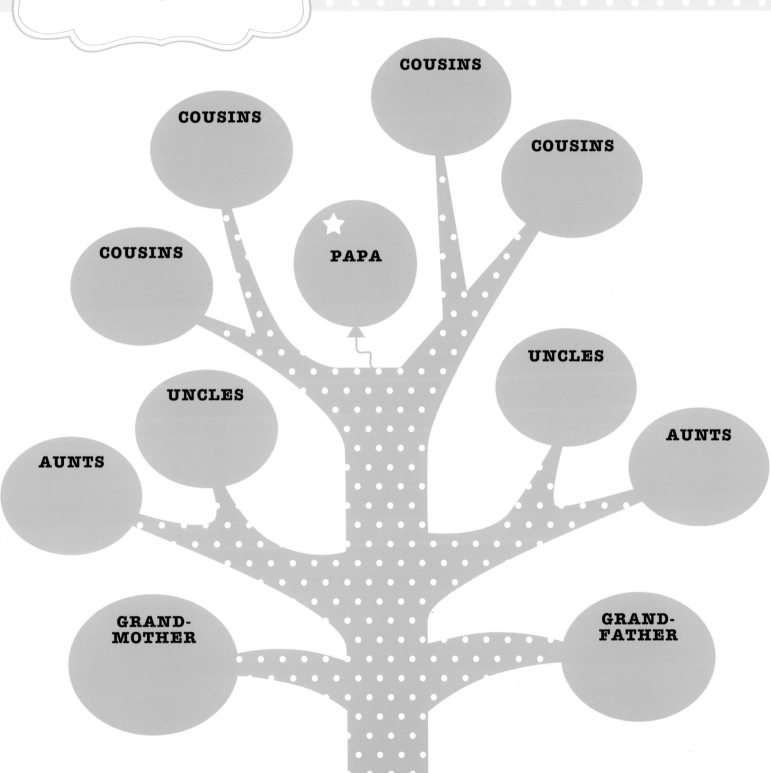

Family
photos

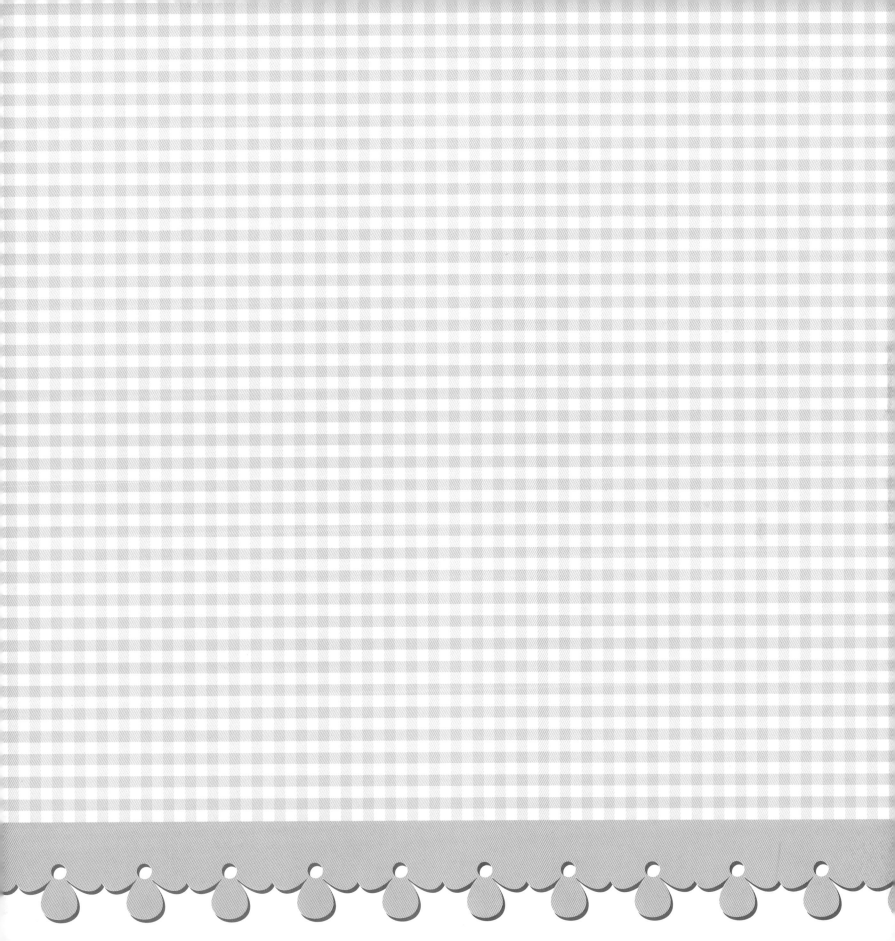

Family photos

I am born!

I was born on

At _____ a.m./p.m.

I weighed _____ pounds/kilogrammes

I was _____ inches/centimetres tall

I was born in

Mama and Papa describe my first day like this:

The most vivid recollection of that day

THE FIRST PHOTOGRAPH OF ME

What they said about me...

Mama's first words were

_____

Papa's first words were

_____

The reactions of my siblings, cousins, grandparents, uncles, aunts and friends:

_____

I also received best wishes from

_____

_____

_____

_____

Precious mementos

A LOCK OF MY HAIR

MY HOSPITAL ID BRACELET

My name

Mama's and Papa's favorite names were

The name they decided on is

They chose this name because

My name means

My nickname is

They call me this because

My portrait

My eyes are

My hair is

Distinguishing marks

How I take after Mama

How I take after Papa

They say I also look like

An unforgettable date

This is what was happening in the world when I was born

The headlines on the front page of the newspaper

The no. 1 song on the charts was

Mama and Papa's favorite singers were

The most famous actors were

Some sports champions of the time

A quart of milk cost

A newspaper cost

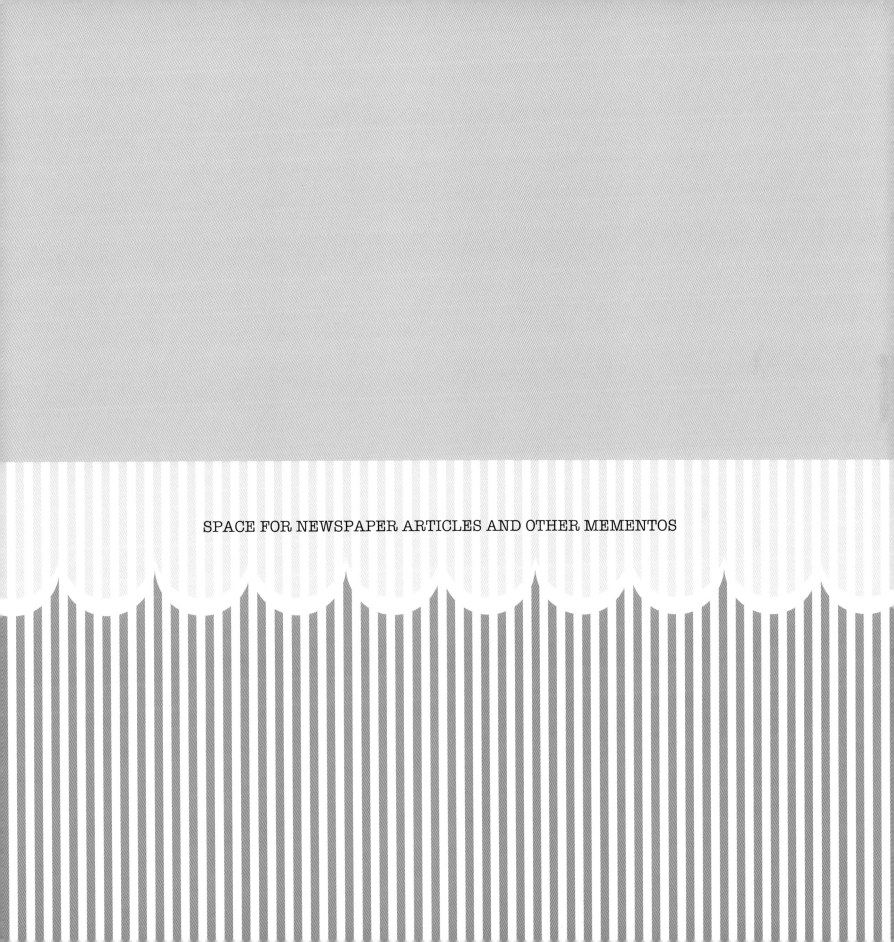

SPACE FOR NEWSPAPER ARTICLES AND OTHER MEMENTOS

Home at last!

The date I arrived at home _____

My first address: _____

_____

During the trip, I _____

_____

_____

Waiting for me at home _____

_____

_____

As soon as I was inside, I _____

_____

_____

My photos

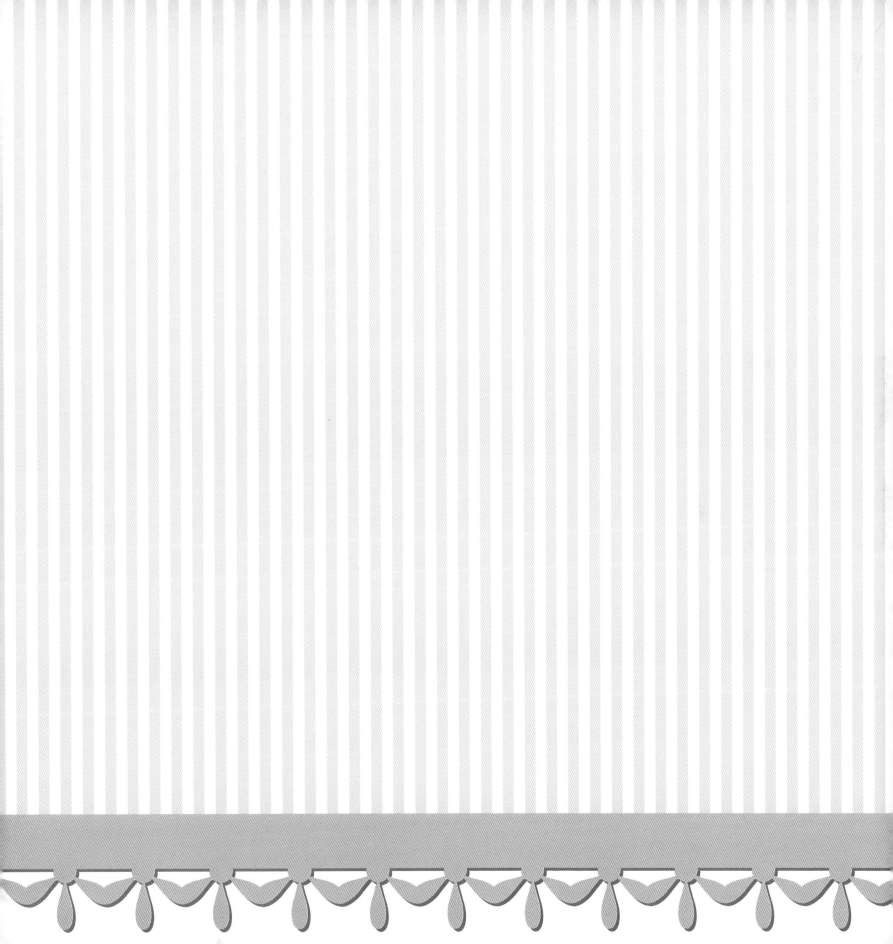

My little bedroom

My bedroom is decorated like this:

_____

_____

_____

_____

Around me were gifts from persons dear to me

_____

_____

_____

_____

_____

_____

_____

Sweet dreams!

My first night at home I slept _____ hours _____

And my parents slept _____ hours _____

That first night they thought _____

_____

To fall asleep I need _____

_____

My favorite lullaby is _____

_____

The position I sleep in _____

_____

I can't fall asleep if _____

_____

_____

My photos

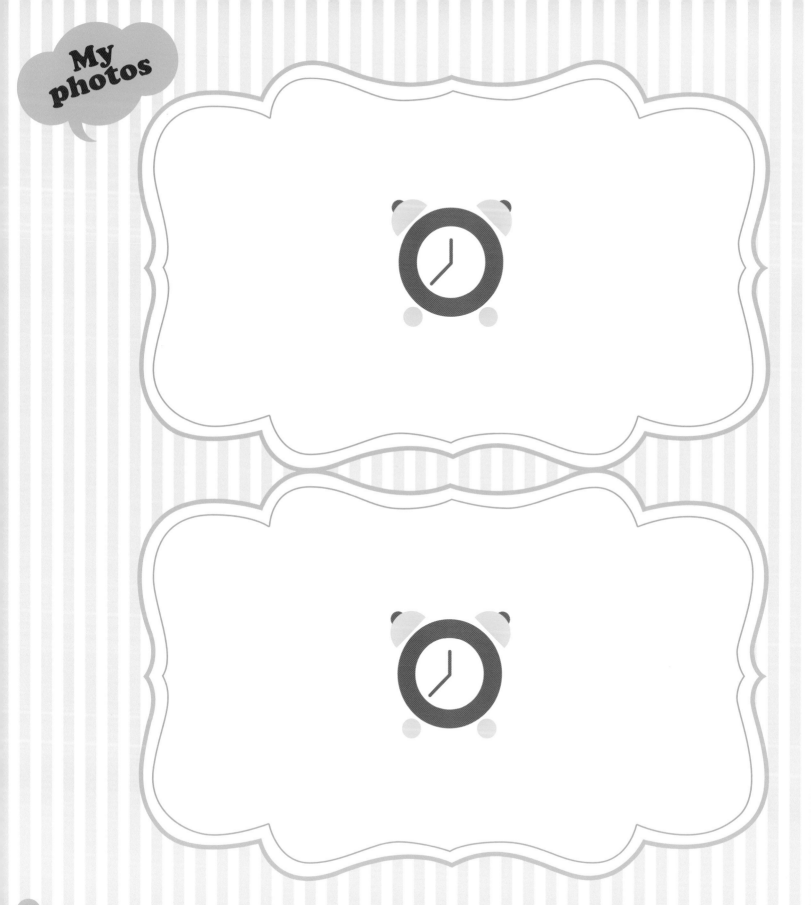

Wake up, sleepyhead!

Am I an early riser or a sleepyhead?

_____

_____

_____

This is how I tell everyone I'm awake:

_____

_____

_____

_____

As soon as I open my eyes, I immediately want

_____

_____

_____

_____

It's time to eat!

My first solid food

Mama's recipes

My favorite dish

I really don't like

I used a spoon all by myself when I was

My
photos

It's bath time

My first time in water

_____

_____

_____

_____

My reactions

_____

_____

_____

_____

In the water I enjoy

_____

_____

_____

_____

My
photos

I grow so fast

1 MONTH	height _____ weight _____
3 MONTHS	height _____ weight _____
6 MONTHS	height _____ weight _____
9 MONTHS	height _____ weight _____
1 YEAR	height _____ weight _____

The first little tooth erupted when I was
_____

_____

This is how I reacted:
_____

_____

At the doctor

My pediatrician

During the first visit, I

The first time I got sick

Discovering the world!

The first family stroll was

This was my reaction:

The persons I met said the following about me:

My favorite places are

My family's first vacation

My
photos

My
photos

The first time that...

I recognized Mama and Papa

I raised my head

I smiled

I slept all night long

I clapped my hands

I discovered my tiny feet

I sat down all by myself

I traveled in a car

I traveled by train, plane or ship

I saw the sea

I touched snow

Taking my first steps

I began to crawl

I stood up all by myself

I began to walk with some help

I walked for the first time all by myself

Look who's talking!

My first word was

The first time I said "Mama" and "Papa"

Here are my very own words that I used to indicate certain objects

My photos

I like this so much!

My favorite toy

My favorite book

I smile every time I hear this song

The thing that makes me happy most of all

The thing that makes me angry most of all

What soothes me

A special day

The event

Those who took part

How I behaved

A particular impression

My photos

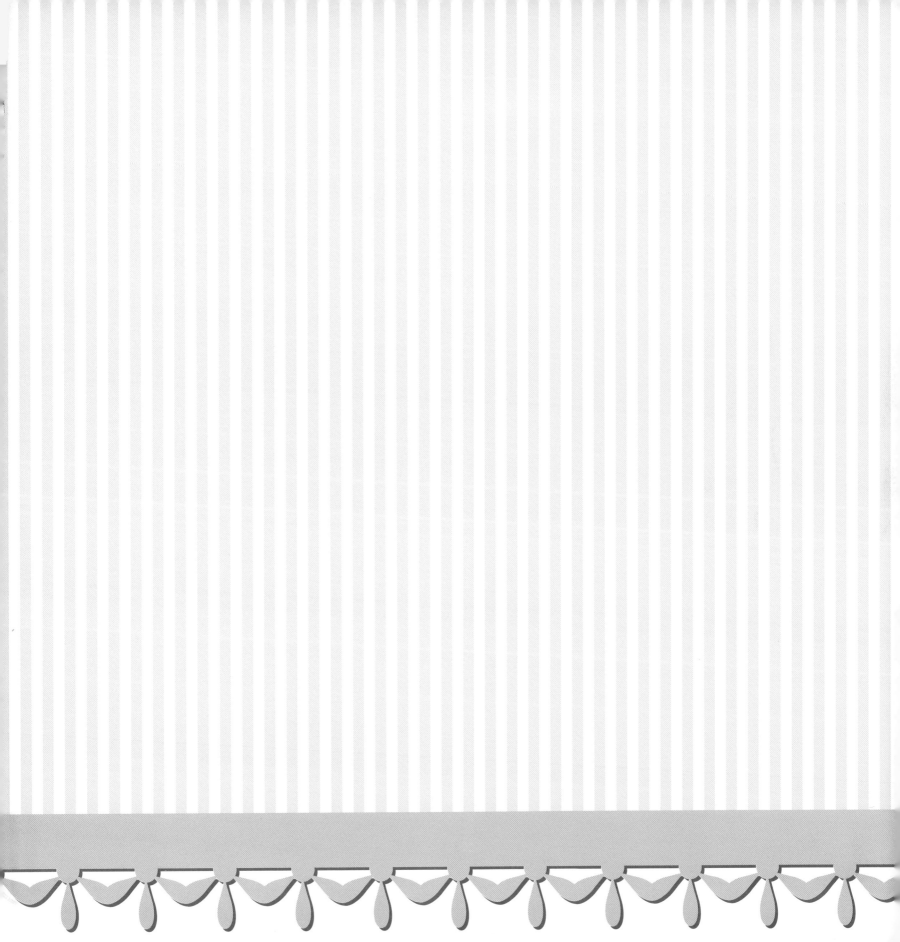

My first birthday

The date and venue of the party

_____

The guests

_____

_____

_____

The presents I received

_____

_____

_____

_____

A special recollection

_____

_____

_____

My
photos

My
photos

An unforgettable year

The moments of the first year of my family that Mama and Papa will never forget

Design
MARINELLA DEBERNARDI

Editorial assistant
GIADA FRANCIA

PHOTO CREDITS

All photographs are by Shutterstock.

WHITE STAR PUBLISHERS

WS White Star Publishers® is a registered trademark
property of De Agostini Libri S.p.A.

© 2015 De Agostini Libri S.p.A.
Via G. da Verrazano, 15 - 28100 Novara, Italy
www.whitestar.it - www.deagostini.it

Translation: Richard Pierce

ISBN 978-88-544-0922-4
1 2 3 4 5 6   19 18 17 16 15

Printed in China